ALL I WANT IS YOU

ALL I WANT IS YOU

A collection of Christian reflections

SANDY MILLAR

Compiled and edited by Mark Elsdon-Dew

Alpha

Alpha International
London

ISBN 1 904074 77 4

Editor's acknowledgements

The production of this book has required the transcribing of
many of Sandy Millar's talks and I would like to express my
thanks and appreciation to all those involved. At my right
hand throughout the book's progress have been Ana
Lehmann and Sharon Hayles, who have worked tirelessly
towards its completion. Many thanks also to John
Valentine, Simon Downham and Jo Glen who read through
the text and kindly made suggestions. Finally, my thanks to
Sandy himself, who only discovered we were planning this
book in its latter stages and kindly gave his permission for
us to go ahead.

Published by Alpha International
Holy Trinity Brompton
Brompton Road, London SW7 1JA

'I am my beloved's and my beloved is mine.'

Song of Songs 6:3

Contents

Contents

THE BISHOP OF LONDON

Sandy's countless friends will be cheered by the publication of this little book of Christian nuggets in which his own unmistakable tone can clearly be heard. Instead of a massy tome of controversial divinity we have a delightful and unoppressive simplicity which nevertheless packs a Christian punch.

Sandy has developed a remarkable leadership style that has played a crucial role in promoting the growth, first of the church of Holy Trinity Brompton, but now, with the development of Alpha, what must be described as a most significant international missionary agency.

It is characteristic of his teaching as revealed in this book that it is full of real life and focuses on those themes which unite all those who love Jesus Christ rather than harping on the sometimes esoteric subjects which divide us. There is also shrewd advice offered with disarming humility about how to live the good life following the Christian way.

I hope that this book will carry the voice of this gifted Christian leader even further than he has travelled on his many journeys over the past decades of service.

Richard Londin:

Introduction

TO CHURCH LEADERS in Britain and around the world, Sandy Millar is renowned for his extraordinary achievements as a church leader.

In his twenty years as Vicar of Holy Trinity Brompton, he built up the biggest and most influential Anglican church in the country, a church which 'planted' new vibrant congregations all over London and founded the Alpha course, one of the greatest evangelistic enterprises of our generation.

As the years went on, bishops, archbishops, theologians and evangelists of all denominations beat a path to the door of his Knightsbridge vicarage to be welcomed with a cup of tea and a warm smile.

But Sandy's church leadership is not complicated. It is founded upon a simple trust that Jesus Christ is alive today and that the local church community, united in their love for God and one another, is there to proclaim it through words and deeds.

To him, faith is rooted in everyday life – relationships with family and friends, struggles with temptation, handling money, behaviour in the workplace...

'I have a secret to tell you,' he will say *sotto voce* with a gleam in his eye, 'Jesus reigns.' We laugh each time we hear him say it – but we know that he is not joking. It is a truth at the centre of all he says and does.

Another thing: Sandy Millar loves *people* – of all ages, backgrounds and nationalities. Spending time with Sandy is, quite simply, *fun*. One reason is that he enjoys stories so much. Whether talking to an individual or a congregation of thousands, it is not long before he sets off with almost childish delight on a story or anecdote. Sometimes it is to illustrate what he is saying, but often it is for the sheer joy of sharing the story with his friends.

The stories could come from his Scottish upbringing, his time as a barrister in London's law courts, his family life with Annette and the four children, his love of poetry and literature, his experiences of God at work – anything he has seen, heard or read.

Many stories come from his time attending conferences in California where he saw a new model of worship and ministry under the leadership of John Wimber which excited him like nothing he had seen before and which was to have a powerful impact upon his life.

It is Sandy's love of story and anecdote that has given rise to this small volume – only published after some pressure was placed upon its reluctant author by his friends. It is compiled from transcripts of his sermons and writings – and any errors are almost certainly the result of defective editing on my part.

One day there will be a larger book but in the meantime here is an hors d'oeuvre – an introduction to the wisdom and simple faith of a man described by former Archbishop of Canterbury George Carey as 'one of the great Christian leaders of our time.'

Mark Elsdon-Dew
Holy Trinity Brompton
May 2005

17

ALL I WANT IS YOU

All I Want Is You

SOME YEARS AGO I was at a conference in California. We had had a wonderful evening and the Spirit of God had been moving all over the place. When it was over, I went for a long walk along the ocean.

As I was walking I was caught up with the excitement of all that lay ahead and just the thrill of the Spirit of God. I was saying, 'Lord, I will give you anything you want... I will do anything you want me to do.' Have you ever said that to him?

And I confess I was rather immodestly listing one or two of the things I thought he might want me to do – to contribute to the kingdom of God. It wasn't a very long list for obvious reasons.

I can honestly claim to have only heard the Lord speak about three times in this way, but as clearly as I have ever heard him speak, he said, 'All I want is you.'

I found that really hard to take. Because I can cope with people who are cross with me, offended or upset. What's much harder is to see this love from Jesus, and yet we let him down again and again. And all he wants is us – all of us. It was the most humbling thing. I thought, 'Oh Lord, is that really right?'

We have got ourselves so worried. We see our value to God in terms of our ministry, or our contribution, our this or our that. When we think about it honestly on our knees, we really can't think about anything that would be of much value to him who owns everything in the whole world. He can raise up people out of the stones if he wants them. He can do anything he likes. But all he wants is you.

Reformation or Revolution

WHEN I WAS AT university we used to have lunch in a particular restaurant every now and again. One of the things that occurred on the menu every Thursday was 'Lamb Cutlet Réforme'. The chef was very sensitive about the feelings of his customers and he would leave a book at the door asking us to leave our comments in it. A friend of mine, who was rather bolder than I was, wrote very simply, 'Lamb Cutlet Réforme will not do. Only a revolution would have saved mine.'

That is actually the Christian message. It isn't reformation we are looking for. It is a revolution in the heart that changes the inside and fills us with a love for God that gives us a love for every creature that he made.

Peace and Joy

JESUS DIDN'T DIE to make us peaceful; he died to reconcile us to God. Once we are reconciled to God we are at peace. He didn't die to make us feel good or happy. He died that we might be forgiven. Once we are forgiven we begin to feel good and at peace. They are by-products of the relationship.

Cooperating with God

YOU MAY REMEMBER the moment in the life of Moses as he led the Israelites towards the Red Sea[1]. He had some pretty restless and grumbling Israelites with him and some very hostile Egyptians behind him.

In front of him lay a vast expanse of water which was impassable and the children of Israel told him to go and find out from God what they were to do. We don't know what Moses said to God, except that the Lord asked him, 'Why are you crying out to me?' which gives us a hint.

[1]Exodus 14.

And then God told him to take his staff and stretch it out over the water. I don't know about you, but if I had been Moses I think I would have said, 'Lord, I don't think you understand the seriousness of this situation. The Israelites want to know what I am to do and all I've heard so far is to hold my stick out over the water.' But then, as it seems to me, what the Lord was saying was, 'If you'll do what you can do, Moses, I will do what only I can do.'

And it's the same with ministry. If you will do what you can do, then God will do what only he can do. So we lay our hands on someone – which is something we can do – and pray that God will do in their lives what only he can do.

Grace

I HAD AN OLD ethics teacher at Durham who used to give us a definition of sin: 'Sin is the difference between what you are and what you might have been.' Grace shows us the same thing. I often use a time of worship to consider where I might have been if God hadn't picked me up, rescued me, and given me what I need to resist temptation and go his way. Recalling it leads to praise, thanks and adoration.

The Patient
and the Parson

SOME YEARS AGO I went to take a communion service in the Brompton Hospital. We were responsible for the chaplaincy there and although I wasn't the chaplain, I was standing in for him that morning. I went into a ward where there were five or six women in bed and I think I must have offended the proverb that says, 'Do not greet your neighbour too cheerily early in the morning.' It was about 8am and I said with a great smile, 'Good morning!'

This young woman sitting on a chair in front of me hardly looked up. 'I've got an 'elluva 'eadache,' she said.

We had just been reading the New Testament together as a staff, so I said to her, 'Would you like me to pray for you?'

Her response showed me how distanced the Church is from so many people in the world today, for I was wearing a dog-collar and a cassock.[1] But she looked shocked at the suggestion that I should pray for her and

---

[1]When I was first ordained I was offered the choice of a black cassock or a grey one and, as I like a bit of colour, I chose a grey one!

turned to a much older woman who was in a bed on my left and said to her in disbelief, ' 'e wants to pray for me.'

I was taught at theological college that if you are going to minister in a hospital you are wise to try to discover who is running the ward. And it is very rarely a member of the medical profession. It didn't take long to see that this woman to whom she was appealing was effectively running the ward!

'Well let him,' the woman said.

I wasn't very happy with the thought that I was going to pray for this young woman just on the say-so of the woman running the ward, and so I said to the young one, 'Yes, but would *you* like me to?'

'Yes' she said.

So I had to. I think I had been hoping that she might refuse and then I could have looked good, because I had after all offered to pray for her – although of course she would have been left with her headache. So I started to pray for her and, as I often say, I was like a proverbial swan, trying to look calm on the surface but underneath I was paddling like anything. 'Lord,' I said silently in my heart, 'if ever you healed anyone – and I know you did – would you please heal this woman, because everybody is looking at her and at me and, Lord, you are going to look very foolish if nothing happens.'

I like to think I was more concerned about the Lord looking foolish than myself, but it is of course a close run thing on these occasions. I prayed for her as I remembered reading Jesus having prayed: I rebuked her headache. I don't really know how you speak to headaches but I remembered that Jesus spoke to fevers.[2] So with this thought in my mind, I simply said, 'I speak to the headache and in Jesus' name command it to be gone.'

The young woman started to shake her head and the reason that I remember the story and certainly the reason that I'm telling it now is that God is so kind. She started to say, 'It's going I think, it's going.' She didn't speak to me of course (why should she?) but she spoke to the older woman in the bed and finally after about two or three minutes she said, 'It's gone.'

As I always say to our people, 'Do you think it was easier for me to talk to her and all the other women in the ward after Jesus had healed her headache or before?' Of course after. And although I cannot tell you that she's a fully paid-up, card-carrying member of the Christian Church – I referred her to her local church in the East End of London – I do know that we had one of the liveliest discussions about Jesus Christ that I think I've ever had. It's what the New Testament calls 'Power Evangelism' and we should pray for more of it.

---

[2]He once spoke to his great friend Peter's mother-in-law's fever – that was a potentially tricky pastoral situation if ever there was one. Also Ezekiel spoke to mountains and valleys and indeed dry bones too. I'm not sure how you address them – 'Mr Bone, are you busy?'

Roast Lamb

I REMEMBER THE first time I realised one of our children didn't like roast lamb. I couldn't believe it. I told him to eat up his roast lamb. He looked at me with great wide open blue eyes and said, 'I don't like roast lamb.'

I couldn't believe that anybody didn't like roast lamb. It was a very significant lesson to me because I suddenly realised, as if the Spirit of God was trying to teach me, that we are different. The fact that they are my children and I love roast lamb doesn't necessarily mean that they do.

The Train

A CHURCH IS rather like a train. There are always those at the front of the train, pouring fuel in and egging it on and hoping it will go at 160 miles an hour. Then there are those at the back who are turning every lever in the hope that this thing will stop! And there are those who are moving up and down the corridor at different times, feeling more secure or less secure.

A pastor's function is to be moving up and down the corridor as well, encouraging those at the back and being encouraged by those at the front and just keeping going.

The Same Message

MY WIFE WAS CONVERTED during her first term at St Andrews University, and for ten years she led what I call a conventional Christian Union life. I'm not being rude about it but she couldn't pray with anybody, she couldn't talk to anybody about Christ and she couldn't minister to anybody. Then, ten years later, she was prayed for by a lovely man, who is dead now, called Edgar Trout. He simply laid hands on Annette and prayed for her to be filled with the Spirit, and she took off.

She started praying in another language and she got this desire – springing from inside – to tell people about Jesus. She immediately sent a postcard to everybody she knew, saying, 'Bring a Bible and a tennis racquet and come and hear about Jesus Christ.' She wrote to David MacInnes, who was then a curate at St Helen's, Bishopsgate, and asked him to come and speak at a weekend. She had no idea that that might be inconvenient for him. She just assumed that everybody would want to take part in this great scheme.

I got a postcard. I was twenty-seven years old, I was at the Bar and I was arrogant enough to think that it couldn't do me much harm to go. I knew there was a hidden agenda. I could find one of those two items (not the other quite so easily), but I got them together and went off for the weekend.

The following year she did exactly the same thing. Only this time she asked John Freeth, who was John Collins' curate at Gillingham. She asked him at 24 hours notice and, poor man, he had no time to prepare at all. He kept sort of starting sentences and not finishing them; he'd start a story and couldn't remember the ending...

But I was attracted both to him and to what he was saying – and what fascinated me was that he was saying the same as David had been saying. It was the same Jesus, the same gospel. They were so different – but there wasn't anything different about what they were saying. I gave my life to the Lord that night.

A Tribute

THERE IS A LOVELY story that Neil Armstrong, the first man to go to the moon, paid a visit to the University of Krakow in Poland on his return. He laid a piece of the moon that he had brought back with him on top of the memorial there to the scientist Copernicus and beside it he wrote a very simple notice in red, 'Without you we would never have got there.'

One day, when we see Jesus face to face, I think we shall want to say the same thing to him.

The Light

YOU MAY KNOW the story of the ship cruising in the channel when the Admiral in charge saw a light coming dangerously close to him. So he flashed a message, 'Move over fifteen degrees.'

He got a message back saying, 'You move over fifteen degrees.'

He was very cross and flashed another message that said, 'I am an Admiral. Move over fifteen degrees.'

And back came the message, 'I am an able seaman. You move over fifteen degrees.'

So he sent his third message, furious, 'I am a battleship. Move over fifteen degrees.'

And back came this reply: 'I am a lighthouse. You move over fifteen degrees!'

I think some of us are inclined to treat the Word of God rather like that. We see something that is totally clear and all the ingenuity of human nature sets about trying to find a way round it.

Somebody once asked Mark Twain what he made of the difficult passages in the Bible. 'It's not the difficult passages that worry me' he said. 'It's the easy ones.'

The issue often is how we respond.

Three Things

THE ROMANIAN PASTOR Richard Wurmbrand was in prison for fourteen years just for being a Christian. Four of those years were spent underground in a box. When he was let out of prison his son, Mihai, who had been four when he went into prison, came to meet him at the prison gates.

On the way home conversation was rather stilted so Mihai asked, 'Dad, what have you learned during your fourteen years in prison?'

Wurmbrand's reply was, 'Well, I've almost forgotten my Bible in all that time, but I do know three things: that there is a God; that Jesus is his Son and that love is the best way.'

God's Plan

GOD HAS A VAST eternal plan which he intends to bring into operation through intercessors and prayer. He says, 'I've got this plan. I wonder if anybody will pray it into existence for me?'

So you and I say, 'Lord, well, I'll pray, if I understand what you're trying to do.'

And I think the Lord says, 'Well, that's quite a big issue. I'm running not just Luton, or Manchester, or London. I'm running a country, a continent, I've got a universe or two. I've got the whole of creation I'm trying to run, and you want to understand what I'm trying to do?

'Is there nobody who is willing to pray without insisting on understanding what I am trying to do?'

And a little hand goes up. 'Lord, I will.' And we start to pray in the Spirit. His Spirit inspires our spirit to pray what he wants prayed. And things begin to change.

Pluscarden Abbey

I REMEMBER BEING taken as a child to see Pluscarden Abbey, near Elgin in Scotland. It had been rebuilt from ruins. The prior was explaining to my mother that they were a silent order and didn't speak except once a month on a Saturday.

My mother, who was a very practical woman, said, 'Well, I bet there are a few things said on the Saturday morning when they are allowed to speak.'

This didn't faze the abbot at all. His reply was, 'Well, the calling is divine, but the relationships are human!' I have often had cause to reflect on that wise piece of advice.

The Absent Holy Spirit

DAVID WATSON used to tell the story of the Sunday School class who had been learning the Creed and the great day came when they came into church to recite it in front of the whole congregation. The teacher looked at the first child, 'I believe in God the Father.'

The second child said, 'I believe in God the Son.'

Then there was a ghastly silence. And a little voice piped up from the back, 'Please Miss, the boy who believes in the Holy Spirit isn't here today.'

That's the trouble really – the boy or girl, the man or the woman who believes in the Holy Spirit isn't here today.

Penultimate Healing

WHEN I FIRST started as a curate there was a little group of people who used to pray regularly for the sick. We'd been praying for one person for quite a long time and she died. But they wanted to encourage me so one of the older women in the group reassured me. 'After all,' she said, 'we've been praying for healing and she has really received the ultimate healing.'

But that wasn't what we were praying for. And I'm always trying to encourage us, particularly in the healing ministry, to use language in the same sense that everybody else uses it. By 'praying for healing' I think I know what we mean. So I always say that if I'm ever ill and you kindly offer to come and pray for me, would you please make it clear what sort of healing you're praying for – and if it's ultimate healing, perhaps you could let me know, because I may just want to ask you to postpone that for a bit.

When You Run Out
of Words...

MY WIFE ANNETTE wanted to make sure that I was prayed for to be filled with the Holy Spirit as soon as possible so that I shouldn't have to wait ten years like she had.

So she took me one night to the Metropolitan Tabernacle where Charles Spurgeon preached for so many years. The man speaking that night was David du Plessis, a South African, who at that time had a wonderful ministry with the Roman Catholic Church particularly.

He took us through various verses in the Acts of the Apostles, all about being filled with the Holy Spirit. At the end of his talk I remember him saying, 'I no longer lay hands on each person individually because there are usually too many, but I ask anyone who would like to pray to be filled with the Holy Spirit to come to the front and I'll pray for you all together.'

Annette and I were both up in the gallery – way up at the back of the Metropolitan Tabernacle – and I couldn't wait to get to the front. Annette who had been a Christian for ten years longer than me, knew many people in the hall and kept running into them. They would ask her how she was and who this was (referring to me!). I remember at one point saying to her, 'Come on, we must get to the front.' I suppose I was worried that, if we didn't, David would have gone and presumably the Holy Spirit with him and then we'd all be left high and dry.

David encouraged us simply to ask and gave us the promise of Jesus that if we asked we would receive. I was happy to dare to believe that. There was a party of nuns that started to sing quietly in the Spirit, making what my godly predecessor used to call 'cheerful farmyard noises'. But I wasn't put off by that. It sounded very beautiful. I didn't start to pray in tongues at that time, but I wasn't worried.

I went home to my room (Annette and I weren't married at the time) and I simply knelt down on my bed and started trying to tell God how much I loved him. I was overwhelmed by that sense of love and I started, 'Oh Lord, I really praise you, I really bless you, I really love you.' But I felt that was inadequate so I started again. 'Lord I really really bless you...'

I felt the helplessness of the whole situation. I was at the Bar and large sums of money had been spent trying to help me be articulate – I'm not asking you to decide whether they were well spent or not – but I couldn't even tell the Lord how much I loved him. At that moment I seemed to hear a voice in my head saying, 'What you need is another language, isn't it?'

'That's exactly what I need' I thought. And I found myself starting to pray in a language that I didn't know

– praying in the Spirit, praying in tongues. And on and off I have never stopped...and what a blessing it has been.

Power and Authority

When Jesus had called the Twelve together, he gave them power and authority to drive out all demons and to cure diseases...

Luke 9:1

I SAW THE DIFFERENCE between power and authority one night at a service. We had a woman who brought a dog into the church. Now I love dogs but we don't have a ministry to dogs and this was a horrid dog, a mean-looking one with its ears clipped. The church was packed and I wasn't sure how the dog would react if somebody trod on it by mistake so I said to her, 'I'm very sorry but you cannot bring that dog in here.'

She said, 'I'm going to.'

I don't know what I would do now, but then I found myself saying to her, 'Well, I'm very sorry, but if you bring the dog in here I shall have to call the police and have you and the dog removed.'

She said, 'Go ahead' and continued to walk into the church.

So I had to. Now I'm approaching an age when all

police officers look young, but this was a young policeman. He was about nineteen. But he was wearing the uniform of the Metropolitan Police and, as he walked in, she walked out.

That's authority. He didn't even say anything to her. But of course behind the uniform lies all the resources of the Metropolitan Police and behind that all the Queen's horses and all the Queen's men – not as many as she once had but enough still to deal with a woman and her dog.

The point is that Jesus gave his disciples authority and power. *We* therefore have this authority; let's pray for more power.

An Eternal Investment

JIM ELLIOTT WROTE this just before he died: 'He is no fool who gives what he cannot keep to gain what he cannot lose.' We give as a response to God's love. We give as an investment in the kingdom of God. Anything you want to find in heaven for you to enjoy in eternity, you have to send on ahead.

Everything I Have

JOHN WESLEY USED to say, 'Make all you can, save all you can, give all you can.' As his income went up, instead of his spending going up commensurably, he simply gave away more and more.

So the question is not 'How much should I give?' as if to say, 'The rest is mine and I can do what I like with it.' The question that I think the Bible teaches us is: 'Everything that I have is God's – how does he want me to use it?'

Change Me

WE OFTEN PRAY, 'Lord, change him' or 'change her.' But the emphasis in the New Testament is much more likely to be on, 'Lord, change *me*.' That having happened, our attitude to those around us will change as well.

John Wimber's First Visit

IN 1982 my predecessor as Vicar of Holy Trinity Brompton asked David Watson, who had been his curate in Gillingham years before and was now travelling all over the world, 'Is there anybody that you think we ought to invite here to speak?'

David's reply was, 'Unquestionably John Wimber – if you can get him.'

At that time we'd never heard of John Wimber. He was of course an American who became world famous as the founder of the Vineyard movement.

Often these kind of ministers are willing to come in from Heathrow on their way to somewhere more exotic and give us a few days in central London. And that's exactly what happened with John.

I was asked to organise an evening for all our home group and Bible study leaders as I was in charge of that side of the church at that time. So we assembled in the Spring (the prayer room under the sanctuary of the church) – about eighty of us. I knew everyone there well as I had been on the staff for six years – I knew the names of their husbands or wives, children, pets and everything else.

John gave a talk on healing. I love talks on healing. As I often say, I've got an attic full of notes on talks on healing. But after he'd spoken for about twenty minutes he suddenly stopped and said, 'OK, now we'll have a break for coffee and then we'll come back and *do* some.' I wasn't sure what that meant but we had what I've often called the longest coffee break we've ever had, because I knew that after it we were going to have to get back into the Spring and *do* some healing. It sounds supernatural and the flesh is always suspicious of the supernatural. So I went round encouraging all the people to have some coffee.

'We've had some,' they said.

'Have some more,' I said.

'We've had some more.'

Eventually we went back into the Spring. I had been sitting in the front row for the talk on healing. I thought it would be rather selfish for me to go back there, so I went right to the back of the room behind everybody, so that I could keep a sort of fatherly eye on the flock and make sure that all was well.

John relied, as you may know, very largely on Words of Knowledge. He waited for God to give him specific information about conditions or people and reacted accordingly.

After a few minutes he had a Word of Knowledge about a lady, he said, who was barren and unable to conceive: 'If she'd like to come forward, we would like to pray for her.'

Well I can remember still the sense of embarrassment and anxiety that I felt as he said that. First of all there were only about five or, at the most, six married women in the room and I knew, in so far as you can tell, that not one of them was trying to conceive. By which I mean they were all young couples with mortgages and things just getting going in life.

But the second reason I was embarrassed was that we who live in a sophisticated part of London and attend a sophisticated church don't talk about these things. We don't talk about 'barrenness' or 'conceiving' or these sort of things. We take part in the process, but we don't talk about them – and I imagined that in California they talked of little else. While all these things were going through my mind, Sarah Wright, who was sitting two or three seats away from me, got to her feet and said, 'I think that must be me.'

I think that was the moment when our church began to grow up. Suddenly it became possible for a beautiful woman in a beautiful church in a beautiful setting to say, in front of all her friends, 'All is not well and I would love your help. Please pray for me.'

So she came to the front and John prayed very simply for her. And that model has stayed with us ever since. For I saw on his face something of the compassion and love of God and on her's something of that expectation and faith. John put his hand on her head and very simply *commanded* healing in Jesus' name. It was as simple as that.

On our way home that night I remember saying to Annette, 'If that is New Testament we must go for that.' What I wasn't sure was whether it really was New Testament.

I had picked up at theological college the idea that God doesn't do that sort of thing today and therefore we were very unwise to suggest that he might, because if he didn't do what he doesn't do and we suggested that he did, we would end up with twice the problem we had before.

Well, nine months later Sarah gave birth to a beautiful little boy and I had the immense privilege of baptising him. She and her husband went on to have four more children and her husband went into full-time Anglican ministry.

Intimacy

WHEN I FIRST visited the Vineyard Church in California I discovered that one of their principle values was 'intimacy with God'. So when I came back I started to talk about that as being one of our values too.

One of the very nice members of our congregation at that time took me to one side and said, 'Please don't use the word "intimacy" because we don't use that word in that context.'

So I started talking about 'the closest possible relationship with God' which is quite a mouthful. But after a bit I stopped because what I really meant was 'intimacy' and I think that's what the Bible means for our relationship with God too.

William Law

WILLIAM LAW, the eighteenth century theologian, said, 'If you think and wonder why it is that you're not as holy or as godly or as purposeful as your predecessors, you will conclude upon reflection that it's because you never thoroughly intended it.'

A Servant First

THE ESSENCE OF the service of Christ is relationship. Jesus said, 'You are my friends if you do what I say.' If I stop doing what he says, does that mean I cease to be his friend? I don't think so. But the essence of the friendship is that I *want* to do what he says. I want to *know* what he says and then I want to *do* what he says. I am his servant and I am his servant first and foremost because I am his friend.

The Way

I USED TO THINK it was wonderful when they started an air service from Heathrow to Inverness – but there was still the hassle of getting to Heathrow. It could be an hour and a half to two hours to get to Heathrow and then only about an hour and a quarter to get from London to Inverness.

But with God there is no way to the way. You haven't got to fight for an hour and a half in order to find the way. Jesus is the way and Jesus is here. Jesus is within reach of you as you sit. Wherever you are Jesus is the way and the truth and the life.

Submission

THE BIBLE HAS NOTHING to say to anyone who does not want to submit to the Lordship of Christ except, 'Submit to the Lordship of Christ.' You will have to one day, and it would be much better if you did it today.

Practical Bible Study

WHEN I FIRST CAME to Christ I went to a Bible study and I was full of questions and things that I longed to hear discussed. And more than once I was told, 'Oh, we are not discussing that tonight.'

So I would say, 'What are we discussing tonight?'

I wasn't interested in what we were discussing and I gradually got less and less interested in the group because it seemed to me that they were only interested in studying the Bible for the sake of studying the Bible.

There was I, a living example of the thing they were supposed to be studying the Bible in order to help, but they were no help to me at all.

Lord Shaftesbury

THE NINETEENTH CENTURY Lord Shaftesbury, when a teenager at Harrow, was deeply moved by the sight of a pauper's funeral.

'When I grow up,' he apparently said to himself, 'I am going to work to make sure that such things do not happen.' His life's work is the stuff of legends: legislation, pressure, money. It was all for the alleviation of suffering and poverty so that at his funeral thousands turned out – royalty and beggars, rich and poor – all to show in their own way their gratitude for his life's work and his love for the under-privileged and poor.

'There goes our Earl,' one of the poorest is said to have cried out as his coffin left the church. 'He loved us and we shall not see his like again.'

But why shouldn't we?

The Greatest Evangelist

ST PAUL gets stick. I understand why that should come from *outside* the church. But why inside the church?

St Paul was one of the most fascinating, amazing, cultured, educated men of his or any time. He was probably the greatest evangelist the church has ever seen. He was a teacher, a pastor, a founder of churches. He was a tender-hearted man. His letters burn with indignation when people are caused to sin or fall. He was a man full of love and interest.

As we look at Paul's teaching, we see that it is always divided into two sections. First, he talks about the great doctrines of the Christian life. But then he goes on to *apply* them. He would have been horrified by the suggestion that the Christian faith is just a series of good ideas that might get us through life. The Christian life is intended to be *lived*.

A Domestic Calling

WHEN I WAS AT the Bar, I remember a woman with about four or five children coming into the Crown Court. She was asked what her job was and she said she was a housewife. She was put down as 'unemployed'. Can you believe that? Unemployed? She never stopped working, but because she was not earning 'x' hundred thousand a year and being asked her opinion on television, she was thought to be 'just a housewife', and described as 'unemployed'.

The Spirit at Work

I REMEMBER one night a young man coming up to me at the end of an evening service to ask me to pray for him. So I said, 'I'd love to. What would you like me to pray for?'

Well he said, 'I'm full of lust and I just hate it. Would you pray for me to get rid of it?'

So I put my hand on his head and started to pray for him but then I felt God checking me and so I stopped and asked him, 'Is this something that you really want to be free from?'

So he looked at me as though I was half-witted. He'd come half-way down the church to ask for it and it was very embarrassing for him. It had been a costly thing to do.

'Yes' he said, 'I really want to be free from it.'

So I said, 'Well, who do you think has put that idea into your head?'

'I don't know,' he said.

So I said, 'Well, do you think the devil would want you to be free from lust?'

'No,' he said, 'I don't.'

So we finally agreed that it could only be the Spirit of God that was at work in him, which was a huge boost to his faith. The enemy had almost persuaded him that he was useless to God; that he was no good and the situation was hopeless. But when he began to see that not only had the Spirit of God not finished with him but had barely begun with him, his faith began to rise. And when faith rises anything can happen.

God's Way

FESTO KIVENGERE, the Ugandan Bishop, used to tell a story about when he had been going to speak to thousands of people at a rally in Kampala. He was a tiny bit late and as he left he spoke to his wife in some way which he deeply regretted. But he was too late to put it right and he had to go.

His car was waiting for him and as he sunk back into the seat he said, 'Now, Lord, please come with me to this rally in Kampala because I want to bring blessing to lots of people.'

But the Lord said to him, 'What about your wife? You must go back and apologise.'

He replied, 'Lord, I'm late. I honestly haven't time, but I will apologise when I get back.'

So the Lord gave Festo a choice. He said, 'You go on to Kampala on your own and I will stay with your wife. Or you go back and apologise to her.'

So he said to the driver, 'I've forgotten something. We

must go back.' So back he went and apologised to her. And the Lord and he went on to the rally and it was a great blessing.

God's Ministry

I ENCOURAGE ALL our people to surrender what they call 'their ministry' and receive *his* ministry. Because if you think of yourself as having a ministry, you'll get exhausted very quickly just by the thought of it.

One of the most moving stories I ever heard John Wimber tell was when he was lying on a hotel room bed, sick and tired of life. He'd visited hundreds and hundreds of churches. He was a church growth expert; he'd studied them all very carefully; he'd written them all up; he'd sent notes to them about pastors and ministers and about what they ought to do. And he was lying, discouraged and worn out, on his hotel bed. And he suddenly heard the Lord speak to him. And what the Lord said to him was, 'John, I have seen your ministry, and now I am going to show you mine.'

And something in his heart thought, 'Yes, Lord, that's much better.'

A Spiritual Perspective

I REMEMBER reading some years ago the words of an expert describing the difference between a Renaissance picture that is Christian and a Renaissance picture that isn't. The difference is that your eye in the Christian picture is always drawn to the figure of Christ. He may not be geographically in the middle of the picture – for example a manger scene where the baby and the manger could be right over on one side – but *every eye in the picture is drawn towards him*.

That is what our worship is aiming at.

An Audience with Royalty

I AM OLD ENOUGH to have been present at the Coronation. I wasn't very old, but I was there. I had a seat on the Mall. It poured with rain and we got soaking wet. After the Queen had been crowned, all the carriages came back down the Mall and the whole crowd of us swarmed from Admiralty Arch down the Mall to outside Buckingham Palace. It was the best-natured crowd I had ever been in. We were all shouting with great enthusiasm, 'We want the Queen!' Every now and then she would come out on to the balcony and wave, and we would go mad. Then she would go back in again and we would take up our shout again.

Imagine for a moment if some uniformed flunky had come out of the palace and through the gates, made his way through the crowd and walked straight up to me and said, 'Mr Millar, Her Majesty would love a word with you. Would you like to follow me?'

Imagine I follow him through the crowd and through the iron railings and through the front door and through the passage and along carpets and carpets and carpets. Imagine there is the Queen sitting at the end of the room and we get nearer and nearer. Then there I am. But imagine I am still shouting, 'We want the Queen! We want the Queen!'

I think she might say, 'It is all right. I am here.'

It is the same with worship. Often there is a sense of the nearness of God when he says, 'I am here.' That is not a time to sing 'On Jordan's banks the Baptist's cry…' but for us to say, 'Oh God, oh God, oh God.'

A Bargain with God

SOMEBODY ONCE ASKED John Wimber, 'Is it all right to make a bargain with God?'

His reply was, 'Yes – if you keep it.'

Marital Conflict

THERE WAS AN ARTICLE in *The Times* headed: 'Wedded Bliss and The Trouble with Marriage'. It had a sub-heading 'To love, honour and argue' and was based upon a new survey which found that thirty-five per cent of couples argue more than once a week. Here is my six-point plan for peace:

1. When issues arise, decide to stop arguing. That needs a decision. Our friends Charlie and Serena Colchester have a wonderful rule which I commend to you. The rule allows any party – husband or wife – to plead the 'Colchester rule' which is: 'I think it is half-past nine – can we discuss this some other time?' What this means is, 'I don't trust myself to discuss this at the moment in the way

that I think the New Testament encourages me to do.' But you have to agree at once when you are going to discuss it.

2. Discover what you are arguing about. It is worth spending a moment working that out. It may or may not be about the sock or the education.

3. Decide to communicate. That means don't sulk, bang pots on the cooker, slam the door, bang the telephone down.

4. Decide to pray. You may just hear what God is saying. Decide to pray together. Decide to pray separately for each other.

5. If you can – humbly, honestly, lovingly – resolve the issue together.

6. If you genuinely can't, then husbands, love your wives as Christ loves the church. And wives, with your husbands, be understanding as to what the will of the Lord is, and choose to submit. That way you will bring enormous glory to God and extraordinary freedom and joy to your husband, your children but, even more important, to you.

The Mandate

SOMEBODY ONCE ASKED the Duke of Wellington whether Christians should be evangelising or not. The Duke, who was wonderfully direct, said, 'What are your orders?'

And one of the keen Christians said, 'Well, we are told to go out and make disciples of all nations.'

'Very well,' said the Duke, 'Obey your orders.'

The Sadness of Sin

MUCH THE MOST common reason for losing that sense of the closeness of Jesus is sin. William Cowper was a lawyer who wrote the hymn 'Oh! for a closer walk with God' which you may know...

Oh! for a closer walk with God,
A calm and heav'nly frame;
A light to shine upon the road
That leads me to the Lamb!

Where is the blessedness I knew
When first I saw the Lord?
Where is the soul-refreshing view
Of Jesus, and his word?

What peaceful hours I once enjoy'd!
How sweet their mem'ry still!
But they have left an aching void,
The world can never fill.

Return, o holy Dove, return,
Sweet messenger of rest;
I hate the sins that made thee mourn,
And drove thee from my breast.

The dearest idol I have known,
Whate'er that idol be;
Help me to tear it from thy throne,
And worship only Thee.

So shall my walk be close with God,
Calm and serene my frame;
So purer light shall mark the road
That leads me to the Lamb.

William Cowper (1731-1800)

I think it is a brilliant expression of the sadness and
frustration brought by sin. The Spirit speaks to us in our
prayers: 'What about this? What about that? What
about this tendency, that relationship? It is spoiling your
life.'

The Christian Life

FOR JOHN WESLEY, the great discovery of his life was 'the Christian life'.

He was the son of a clergyman so he knew a bit about the Christian faith. But in his postgraduate days in Oxford he was orthodox in belief, religious in practice, upright, full of good works, visited prisons and workhouses, gave food, clothing and education to slum children. He observed Saturday and Sunday as a Sabbath, he went to church, took holy communion, gave money, searched the scriptures, fasted and prayed.

But he said later that he had been 'bound in the fetters of my own religion, trusting in myself – that I was righteous – instead of putting my trust in Christ'.

A few years later he came to trust in Christ, in Christ only, for salvation and he received an inward assurance that his sins had been forgiven. In 1738 he wrote, 'I had even then the faith of a servant though not that of a son' – which is what he came to have later.

His great message for the rest of his life was that the key to the Christian life was to remember that what we *do* comes from what we *are*.

Come to Christ

MALCOLM MUGGERIDGE came to speak at Holy Trinity Brompton twice I think. He had been deeply affected by Mother Teresa when he was in India and had become a Christian. He was a journalist and very bright. And whenever he came here he would speak for about thirty-five minutes.

I remember him saying, 'I used to be invited to speak all over the world, but I don't get invited now because my message is always the same, "Come to Christ".

"Mr Muggeridge, what is the issue facing the Russians?"

"They must come to Christ."

"What about the South American republics?"

"They must come to Christ."

"The Palestinians, the Israelis?"

"They must come to Christ." '

So you could see why he wasn't invited any more. They wanted to have a great intellectual discussion and he wasn't into that by then.

A Helping Hand

ST AUGUSTINE ONCE SAID, 'If I fall into a well, please don't peer over the top and ask me if I know how I got in there. Just help me out, will you?'

It is not for the Church to say, 'How did you get into that mess?' Instead, the Church should say, 'Would you like a hand?'

A Sincere Devotion

THE CALL OF GOD is a strange thing. You start to analyse it and you get lost. You try to describe it to an old friend who is outside the kingdom of God and he looks blank and suggests a game of golf next Sunday. Nevertheless, it is a real and precious thing. It is the stirring in every part of us – mind, body, soul and spirit – in response to the overwhelming love of God.

Jesus spoke to Nicodemus about the wind that 'blows wherever it pleases. You hear its sound, but you cannot tell where it comes from or where it is going. So it is with everyone born of the Spirit.' (John 3:8) Nicodemus looked blank too because until then it hadn't happened to him and he couldn't therefore see the kingdom of God.

For some it is a gradual realisation; for some quite a sudden thing (there are examples in the Bible of both). But in all of us who have been born from above, something distinctive has happened. Paul describes it beautifully in 2 Corinthians 11 when he says we have been drawn to a 'sincere and pure devotion to Christ'.

Spiritual Maturity

THE TEST OF spiritual maturity is not the ability to speak in tongues, prophesy, memorise or expound Scripture.

It is the ability and willingness to serve God and others through good works; it is learning to love and serve the unlovely; it is valuing those whom the world has discarded.

God's Hands and Feet

THERE IS AN OLD poem I love which goes like this:

Christ has no hands but our hands to do His work today,
He has no feet but our feet to lead men in His way,
He has no tongue but our tongue to tell men how He died,
He has no help but our help to bring them to His side.
We are the only Bible the careless world will read,
We are the sinner's gospel, we are the scoffer's creed,
We are the Lord's last message, given in deed and word.
What if the type is crooked? What if the print is blurred?
What if our hands are busy with other work than His?
What if our feet are walking where sin's allurement is?
What if our tongues are speaking of things His lips would
spurn?
How can we hope to help Him and hasten his return?

Annie Johnson Flint (1866-1932)

Spiritual Perception

TO ATTEMPT TO DISCERN the Spirit with the flesh is like an attempt to describe the sunset with algebraic equations – it simply can't be done.

Saving Souls

SOME YEARS AGO a friend of mine said something that I have never forgotten: 'If the American railroad companies in the 1930s had been interested in the transportation of people, they'd have bought aeroplanes.' But they weren't.

And I have to say that if the Church of Jesus Christ was interested in the salvation of souls, there would be a great deal that they would do differently today.

What about Baptism?

MY FIRST PRESBYTERIAN minister said from the pulpit one day, 'The only "ism" that does not lead to hell is rheumatism!' I was frightfully pleased with that and said it once in one of the Sunday morning church services. When I got home one of my children said, 'What about baptism?'

Lego

I HAVE OFTEN SAID that if I ever met the inventor of Lego I would try to express my gratitude to him because for hours and hours our children played with Lego which enabled me to get on with something else.

It is no good telling children to sit still and 'be good'. You can't do it. And Jesus didn't say to the Church, 'Sit still and be good until I return' because he knows we can't do it either. He has work for us to do.

Christin You

THERE WAS ONCE a gorilla at Edinburgh Zoo who died. This was a major crisis because there was a bank holiday coming up on the Monday and they had no gorilla. At that time a chap who wanted a job went to the zoo and said, 'Have you got a job for me?'

And they said, 'Amazing, wonderful, our gorilla's just died and we would love you to be the gorilla. Here is a skin and here is a gorilla helmet and you've got three days to practise. When the crowds come on Monday you'll be able to do it.' So he was thrilled with this and he put on the skin and the gorilla head and he practised all Saturday and Sunday.

By Monday morning he was very proficient at swinging away on the bars in a very impressive way. That day masses of people came to watch him. But he got caught up with enthusiasm while swinging on the bar and at one point gave an extra little hop, just to prove to the crowds that he could do it. And to his horror he found himself sailing out over the top of his cage into the next-door cage, which belonged to the lion.

He landed with a thump about ten feet away from the lion, who got up and started moving towards him. At this moment our friend's nerve broke and he started shouting, 'Help! Get me out of here quick, help, help!'

And with the lion just inches away, he felt a furry voice in his ear say, 'Shut up or we'll both lose our jobs!'

This little story raises the issue of what makes a gorilla: is it the inside or the outside? And what makes a Christian? Is it the inside or the outside?

A Woking Sermon

I REMEMBER A MISSION we did at Woking. At one of the supper parties there was a young computer operator who was very nice. He lectured me for about twenty minutes about the Christian faith, which was fine except he didn't know anything about it at all. He said to me, 'Of course I really love the Sermon on the Mount.'

And I said, 'Which bit of the Sermon on the Mount do you like?'

'Well, I just love Jesus' teaching. He was such a wonderful teacher.'

This went on for quite a bit of time and then I said to him, 'Do you like the bit at the end?'

And he said, 'Which bit is that?'

So I said, 'Well, you know, when Jesus says that those who do my words are like wise people and those who don't are like foolish ones who will be destroyed.'

He said, 'I don't like that bit at all.'

So he came to the conclusion that he didn't like the Sermon on the Mount after all.

A Broken Heart

ON A TRIP TO Poland I met a dear lady. She was about seventy-five, dressed in black and with a wrinkled brown face. We were in a conference hall of about 3,500 people. This lady came up and the interpreter said, 'She wants you to pray for her left eye,' which was twitching. We hadn't much time because there were a lot of people.

I looked at her left eye and I asked the Spirit of God to come and do whatever he wanted to do for her. Into my head came the question, 'How long have you had that?'

She replied, 'About two years.'

I said, 'Did something happen two years ago?'

'My husband died.'

And it became perfectly clear to me that her twitching left eye was a symptom of a broken heart. Into my head came God's promise, 'I will bind up the broken hearted.' I said, 'Lord, would you bind up her broken heart.'

As we prayed, the Spirit of God ministered to her heart. Her eye stopped twitching (that's the least of it, in a sense) and she was put into touch with God in a way that she had never been before. I left her in seventh heaven. Her eye stopped twitching when her heart was healed.

A Life Worth Living

THE CHRISTIAN LIFE is an adventure – much the most exciting adventure you could ever be involved in. After all, Everest has been conquered. The Atlantic has been rowed across in both ways. Much the most challenging adventure is a Christian life – doing what God has called you to do.

The Trapped Angel

DO YOU KNOW the story of Michelangelo standing in front of a huge block of marble? They said to him, 'What are you looking at?'

He replied, 'I see an angel trapped and I intend to release him.'

Jesus was the same with the woman caught in

adultery in John, Chapter 8. He didn't see a woman with sins and a past. He saw a woman with a future and a hope and he alighted on that, as he does with you and with me.

A Prayer Revival

THE EVANGELISATION of the world depends upon a revival of prayer. Prayer is the life blood of the people of God. The New Testament lays a greater stress on prayer than it does on the evangelisation of people. There is a deeper need to pray than there is even for people to be converted, and I don't say that lightly because there is a fierce need for conversion. But conversions won't happen unless we are praying and the Bible says that from beginning to end.

It is not because there is magic in prayer. The reason is the relationship with God, of which prayer is an expression. Of course prayer doesn't achieve anything in itself – it is God that achieves it, but through the relationship we have with him in prayer.

Love

If I speak in the tongues of men and of angels, but have not love, I am only a resounding gong or a clanging cymbal. If I have the gift of prophecy and can fathom all mysteries and all knowledge, and if I have a faith that can move mountains, but have not love, I am nothing. If I give all I possess to the poor and surrender my body to the flames, but have not love, I gain nothing.

Love is patient, love is kind. It does not envy, it does not boast, it is not proud. It is not rude, it is not self-seeking, it is not easily angered, it keeps no record of wrongs. Love does not delight in evil but rejoices with the truth. It always protects, always trusts, always hopes, always perseveres.

Love never fails. But where there are prophecies, they will cease; where there are tongues, they will be stilled; where there is knowledge, it will pass away. For we know in part and we prophesy in part, but when perfection comes, the imperfect disappears. When I was a child, I talked like a child, I thought like a child, I reasoned like a child. When I became a man, I put childish ways behind me. Now we see but a poor reflection as in a mirror; then we shall see face to face. Now I know in part; then I shall know fully, even as I am fully known.

And now these three remain: faith, hope and love. But the greatest of these is love.

1 Corinthians 13

I OFTEN THINK of the man who went off as a missionary to Africa and used to read this chapter to himself every morning. As he was praying he substituted his own name for the word 'love': 'James is patient,

James is kind. He does not envy, he does not boast...'

And he would see how far he could get until the Spirit of God said to him, 'What about last night?', 'What about yesterday?' And he was driven back to his knees to pray for a contrite heart.

Give it Up

THE POINT OF LENT is not just to give up coffee or alcohol or whatever it is we have resolved, worthy though that may be. It is to give up sin.

A New Morality

THERE IS NOTHING NEW about the so-called 'New Morality'. Sometimes younger people look at me and say that I am out of touch and old-fashioned. If I may say so, if you have fallen for the 'New Morality', it's you that's old-fashioned. Because the 'New Morality' is the old immorality by another name.

The people of God were always tempted to pervert God's will and immorality and godlessness have always gone together.

So it's no coincidence that with the lessening of the impact of the Christian faith over the last twenty-five to thirty years and the growth of a rather arrogant paganism that seems to think it can exist without God's love, protection, power and grace, the brazenness of the new immorality has increased.

An Absence of Sentimentality

SHORTLY AFTER I gave my life to Jesus Christ, and long before I was ordained, I found myself browsing on a barrow in a street market. There I came across an old second-hand copy of *My Utmost for His Highest* by Oswald Chambers.

I paid the two shillings demanded and brought it triumphantly to show Nicholas Rivett-Carnac who was running the church at Holy Trinity Brompton then.

'Is this all right?' I asked.

'Gold!' he replied.

And so it has proved to be – not to all, I'm sure, but to me. One reason, I think, is his total absence of sentimentality in what he says about our relationship with God. Let me quote to you a little of what he writes:

'We shall all feel very much ashamed if we do not

yield to Jesus on the point he has asked us to yield to him... To get there is a question of will, not of debate nor of reasoning, but a surrender of the will, an absolute and irrevocable surrender on that point. An overwhelming consideration of ourselves is the thing that keeps us from that decision, though we put it that we are considering others.'

You see what I mean about an absence of sentimentality?

God's Plan

BISHOP LESSLIE NEWBIGIN used to say to the Church in South India, 'Nobody is entitled to ask God "Where is this going to lead?" ' We are instructed to follow and it will become clear later where it takes its place in God's overall scheme.

Mysterious but True

GOD HAS ALWAYS LOVED us; he always will love us. Jesus' suffering and dying was inspired by love. If he'd only been interested in law and justice he would simply have left us to suffer all the consequences of our evil and helplessly selfish world. But he didn't. As an old divine once wrote:

How you can think so well of us, and be the God thou art,
Is darkness to my intellect, but sunshine to my heart.

The gospel is the good news of God's love in Christ Jesus – mysterious, incomprehensible but...true.

Watchmen

I have posted watchmen on your walls, O Jerusalem;
  they will never be silent day or night.
You who call on the Lord,
  give yourselves no rest,
and give him no rest till he establishes Jerusalem
  and makes her the praise of the earth.

Isaiah 62:6

I WONDER IF GOD made the world in the way that he made it to ensure there is always somebody in the world for whom it is dawn, the sun is rising and their prayers start. It means there are always people who are awake and praising him. We don't have to be up 24 hours a day, which is rather a relief.

But it does mean that when our turn comes and it is the dawn, there are others across the other side of the world who are hoping and relying upon us to pray, that God might be able to say to the angels and all those in heaven, 'Don't you worry about earth. It is in very good hands. I have posted watchmen.'

Caught in the Act

I USED TO SAY in the Sunday services, as you are supposed to do as a clergyman and a pastor, 'Please, please don't speak to anybody you know. Speak to the new people.'

And they would say, 'Yes, absolutely.'

And after the services, guess what? They were all speaking to their friends. As I walked past they would look guilty because they were 'caught' talking to their friends! In fact what was happening was that the Spirit of God was bringing people together and they really loved each other, and on Sunday mornings they really wanted to talk to the people they loved. They had prayed for them last Wednesday and they really wanted to know how they were. I was busy attempting to undo the work that the Spirit of God was doing in bringing them together.

Divine Humour

I OFTEN THINK of the story of the small boy who came to church with his mother and giggled throughout the entire first half of the service. His mother was embarrassed, then she was cross, and then she was both embarrassed and cross, and she felt sure that everybody was looking at her. When they got home she gave him a little talking to and this four-year-old boy replied, 'I am not sure what the difficulty is.'

She said, 'You mustn't giggle in church. It is a solemn place. Everybody was looking at you. The minister was looking at you.'

'Well,' he said, 'I'll tell you what it was. I told God a joke – and he and I were laughing about it.' Which rather flummoxed her theology. She had been brought up in a different era and she hadn't realised that it is possible for children to tell God jokes and for God to love them – both the children and the jokes – even if the parents don't.

Born from Above

'YOU MUST BE born from above' was said to be John Wesley's favourite text. Someone asked him once why it was that he chose so often to speak on that verse.

'Because,' he replied, 'you must be born from above.'

Black Bulls

HAVE YOU EVER walked through a field with others and seen two big black bulls in the middle of the field? There is something about those big black bulls that makes you think it would be wiser to stick together until you get to the other side of the fence.

The fact is that we are surrounded by big black bulls, and worse. And the irony of the whole thing is that there's a sense in which the Lord has either put them there or allowed them to stay there in order to drive us together and teach us.

And we have to say, 'Lord, hang on, you didn't bring us into the middle of a field, did you, with two big black bulls just for them to destroy us and trample on us and threaten us and make us seem stupid?'

And the Lord says, 'No, I didn't. I put you in the middle of the field with two big black bulls so that you might learn to *fight*, to fight, and not be wet.'

The Lord has told us that when we fall into what the Authorised Version calls 'divers temptations and trials', count it all joy. Why? Because you are being brought to maturity. Then instead of falling down into a pile on to the floor and saying 'I give up' you think to yourself 'I *do not* give up. I've realised that the Lord allowed those black bulls to be there so that we should stick together and hold hands and *fight*.'

Hyde Park

BISHOP WINNINGTON-INGRAM, preaching in Hyde Park, was heckled by an older man of the road. 'What about St Paul then?' he shouted. 'He liked a drop when it was good, didn't he?'

'I don't know,' the Bishop replied, 'but when I get to heaven I'll ask him.'

'And what if he's not there?' came back the heckler.

'Then you ask him,' the Bishop responded.

The Five Thousand

Then he took them [the disciples] with him and they withdrew by themselves to a town called Bethsaida, but the crowds learned about it and followed him. He welcomed them and spoke to them about the kingdom of God, and healed those who needed healing.

Late in the afternoon the Twelve came to him and said, 'Send the crowd away so they can go to the surrounding villages and countryside and find food and lodging, because we are in a remote place here.'

He replied, 'You give them something to eat.'

They answered, 'We have only five loaves of bread and two fish.'

But he said to his disciples, 'Make them sit down in groups of about fifty each.' The disciples did so, and everybody sat down. Taking the five loaves and the two fish and looking up to heaven, he gave thanks and broke them. Then he gave them to the disciples to set before the people. They all ate and were satisfied, and the disciples picked up twelve basketfuls of broken pieces that were left over.

Luke 9:10-17

THE FEEDING OF the Five Thousand is the only gospel passage that appears twice in the year in the *Book of Common Prayer* readings – once at the beginning and once at the end. The Reformers were trying to make a point that one of the keys to understanding the Christian faith and relationship is to be found in this story.

It is fascinating to consider the agonies the disciples must have gone through. I don't know at what point it dawned on them that there was a link between the 5,000 men – plus women and children – and these five loaves and two little fish. I don't know whether they all came to the same conclusion at the same minute but, somewhere along the line, it must have occurred to them, 'He's going to ask us to feed them with these five loaves and two fish.' Which is sure enough what he did.

The point is that at every stage two things were operating. One was that Jesus – graciously, wonderfully, kindly – was inviting them to cooperate with him. Secondly he was helping them to see that without him they would fall flat on their faces. You know, I know and everybody knows that you can't feed 5,000 men with five loaves and two fish. Jesus was saying to them, 'We have a wonderful opportunity here. Cheer up, smile, we've got 5,000 hungry people, and we've got five loaves and two fish. Why don't we feed them?'

They said to him, 'You feed them!'

Jesus, it seems to me, was saying, 'Why don't we *both* feed them? We'll do it together.'

Jesus calls us to cooperate and understand that without him we can do nothing. That's why we are so constantly vulnerable. But it's also why the only thing worth holding out for is the ministry of the Spirit. When we talk about a ministry of the Spirit, it seems to me that what we're talking about is cooperation with God.

Windsor Great Park

SOME TIME AGO I found myself walking in Windsor Great Park. I came out through the trees at Smiths Lawn. But instead of the usual idyllic scene (which is practically nothing going on and just mown grass for miles and miles) I came across the most astonishing scene. There were troops everywhere. There were ferret cars, little closed-in mini tanks, and soldiers peering out of bushes and things. One soldier was about ten feet in front of me. I was shocked, I suppose, to see the great scene, so I said in a friendly voice, 'Who's winning?' (I was thinking of old Corps days at school).

He said grimly, 'No one.'

So I said (as I didn't like to leave it like that), 'Where's the enemy?'

To which he replied, 'There isn't one.'

So I said (because I wasn't going to go down totally without firing one more shot), 'Well, what's all this about? An exercise?'

He was beginning to thaw and he said, 'No, a visit.'

'A visit?' I said, 'Who's coming?'

At which he got all conspiratorial, looked both ways, and said in hushed tones, 'The Queen.'

'Ah,' I said. 'The Queen.'

And on that note I walked on and he went back to his

duties. I thought then, and I have thought on occasion since, what an extraordinarily wonderful visual aid that is. The Queen is coming and the whole place comes alive – stiff with activity and people all atuned, getting ready. They were getting ready for the rooting out of evil and I wouldn't have given much for the chances of anyone who had appeared at that moment with evil intent.

That is the very picture that Jesus portrays again and again about the time between his first coming and his second coming. He has set people – his people – to do something so that when he comes (just as when the Queen was coming, only infinitely more so) they are not just lounging around leaning on the end of their rifles but actually watching for sources of evil, anticipating them and willing to act and *do* something, rather than just express views.

A Book for Everyone

THE BIBLE WASN'T WRITTEN for Christians. It was written for everyone – to draw all people to Christ. What the Bible says is not designed just to keep Christians comfortable and happy and well fed. It's to prevent us from going wrong. And therefore we are entitled to speak about what the Bible says as affecting everybody in the world – whether they know it or whether they don't.

Treasure in Heaven

I WAS PREACHING recently on the rich young ruler.[1] You remember how sad he was because he had a great deal of money and he'd heard Jesus say that he should give it all away. But actually of course that wasn't what Jesus was saying at all. There's no point in giving away everything for the sake of it. There's no virtue in poverty.

[1]Matthew 19:16-29

If Jesus had said to him, 'If I were you I'd get your money out of Euro-Disney and put it into Sainsbury's...' the young man would have been thrilled. He'd have got onto his mobile telephone straight away and done it.

But what he failed to see was that that was exactly what Jesus *was* saying to him. 'Get out of stocks and shares...and give to the poor...and you will have treasure in heaven.' How often do we see giving as an *investment*?

Just One Group

WHEN JESUS WAS BAPTISED what was the first thing he did? He formed a small group. There must have been 24,000 people in the temple at Jerusalem probably at one time. So what does Jesus do? He says, 'I can't operate in those sort of numbers. I'm going to form a small group.'

And he got twelve of them and he said, 'Do you want to come with me? We'll have some fun. We'll do some ministry and it's going to be a riot and I will change you and I will form you and correct you from time to time and give you my Spirit and we'll heal the sick and minister to the poor. We'll do everything we need to do and we'll go out.'

The strength of the church is in its groups. And the church service, the 'celebration', is a collection of groups.

A Mature Student

I HEARD THE OTHER day of two young boys coming home from school. The granny of one of them was sitting in a chair reading her Bible.

He was embarrassed and was heard to whisper encouragingly to his friend: 'Don't worry about Granny, she's swotting for her finals.'

Acacia Villas

I'VE ALWAYS HAD this dream that in somewhere I call Acacia Villas, Christians from every sort of background and denomination up and down the street recognise each other and they pool their resources. They swallow their differences.

It doesn't mean that they become uniform. It means that they recognise a unanimity of Spirit which enables them to hold together in order to achieve God's purposes, which is to be salt and light of the kingdom in Acacia Villas so that they do not rest until there is nobody in Acacia Villas who isn't a part of the kingdom of God. That means loving them first of all.

The Greatest in the Kingdom

Jesus called a little child and had him stand among them. And he said: 'I tell you the truth, unless you change and become like little children, you will never enter the kingdom of heaven. Therefore, whoever humbles himself like this child is the greatest in the kingdom of heaven.'

Matthew 18:2-4

NOW ISN'T THAT one of the strangest things that Jesus could have said? How many humble children do you know? I mean humble! As in 'My dad's got a much smaller car than yours…', 'Our team isn't quite as good as yours… '

So I don't think Jesus can have meant that. Then what does he mean? Let me suggest a possibility or two.

1. Children expect to work from someone else's agenda. I still remember one of my earliest regular

questions: 'What am I to put on today?'

That means, 'What's happening today? Is it gardening clothes or smarter? Gumboots or shoes?'

There's an expectation that there is a plan somewhere of which I am a part. The only question is, 'What is it?'

It doesn't take much imagination to see what Jesus is driving at. Paul in his letter to the Ephesians makes it the theme tune of the entire letter. God has a plan. His will, which he purposed in Christ is 'to be put into effect when the times will have reached their fulfilment – to bring all things in heaven and on earth together under one head, even Christ.' (Ephesians 1:10)

So it's working clothes today!

It is astonishing how far the Church has got from this understanding. We seem to think that God's plan for salvation was so that we could be happy. So that we could enjoy contentment, peace, joy, etc, here on earth until the Lord returns and then continue on in this happy state – in heaven too – for ever.

Of course it is nonsense. But it is only possible to think like this at all because it is a half-truth. God does want us to be happy. But we shall only be happy if we find out what he is doing and throw ourselves into that.

Later on in his letter Paul says he is praying for the Christians that God '...may give you the Spirit of wisdom and revelation, so that you may know him better.' (Ephesians 2:17)

That's what we need: to see what the Father is doing, as Jesus did, and do that; to fit in with his plans and be ready to scrap our own – to be like a child.

2. Children are always looking forward. Obvious really! They've nowhere else to look.

But what about us? It means sitting light to the past and being excited about the future even if we don't know what it will bring.

I've noticed in one very small way of my own that I can't get as excited as I once could about photographs of the children when they, we, were young.

We've moved on. Things have changed. I have loved each stage as it has come. The only question now is, 'What next?'

Of course I look back with deep gratitude, wonder and praise to God for all the many ways he has blessed us as a family and as a church in the past. But that is a springboard, a launching pad, to the future.

I encourage all of us of my age and greater to see ourselves as moving towards the dawn – like the Old Testament character Enoch who 'walked with God and was not.' He'd moved, or been moved, on! That means the big C – Change. The graffiti artist was right after all: 'Change is here to stay.'

A Child's Prayer

MANY YEARS AGO I was in California for a conference. Towards the end of my visit I called home and spoke to my wife and all except one of my children. I ended the conversation by confirming the details of my homeward flight, time of arrival and how much I was looking forward to seeing them all the following day. What I didn't realise was that the child I hadn't talked to was distraught.

My long-suffering wife, full of faith, solved the growing household crisis. 'I'll tell you what,' she said to the children, 'let's gather round the kitchen table and ask God to get Daddy to ring us up again.' And that is what they did. 'In Jesus' name, Amen!' they prayed. I, meanwhile, was spending my last day in California at Disneyland. As I came off the Pirate Ship with two or three friends, I was suddenly overcome by an overwhelming sense that all was not well at home. I put it off for about ten minutes. It seemed so stupid. Anyway, I hoped to be home by the end of the next day.

But finally, I could bear it no longer. 'You go on,' I said to my friends, 'I'm just going back to the entrance to telephone home.'

It was quite a business – I had to walk about 400 yards out of my way, get change, stand in a line for about half an hour until I could get to a telephone, and finally get put through to Suffolk. But what rejoicing at the other end! It taught me a very valuable lesson: that God hears when one of his children cries out in Suffolk, and is not only willing but able to communicate that cry – without e-mail, mobile telephone, fax or letter – to another of his children in California.

Let's Look Outward

WITHOUT WISHING to get involved in party politics or racial sensitivities I would love to feel, as a Scot (and as most ex-patriots, fiercely so!), that we could recover the godly instincts that we had 150 years ago and set ourselves to see how we could go out into the world and be a help.

At that time and later, practically every ship had a Scots engineer. There were Scots missionaries, medical workers, teachers all over the world and the world greatly benefited. Now, it seems to me, the wind has changed. The talk is more insular, inward-looking, with an emphasis on governing ourselves.

The same spirit is in the process of overtaking the Church if we don't check it.

But an inward looking, self-protecting and absorbing desire on the part of the Church to concentrate on the well-being of the Church will lead to slow suffocation and death.

A willingness and positive longing on the part of the Church to take responsibility for those around it – the world, the poor, the lost, the marginalised, and the nation – will lead to glory.

An Ethical Issue

SOMEBODY TOLD ME the other day that scientists are now specifically instructed not to exercise ethical considerations in their scientific experiments and work. They are the scientists – it is for other people to consider the ethics. I want to say to them humbly, and with all the strength I can muster, that when they get to heaven and stand before the judgment seat of God that will not be an option.

We are each responsible for what we do. There are ethical issues and there is an ethical dimension to life.

The Question

YOU REMEMBER the Snoopy cartoon? A bearded man in the park with a huge placard: 'Jesus is the answer!' and the little dog running behind with a flag trailing out of his mouth, 'Yes, but what is the question?'

The question is easy to write today. It is everything going on in the world that is so destructive of happiness and hope. The moral vacuum, pain, war, disease, loneliness, pointlessness – why the hell…? Why doesn't God *do* something? The answer is…he has. He came into the world and this world didn't recognise him.

The Distracted Sheep

A FRIEND OF MINE told me that during a time of worship she had seen a picture in her mind. She thought that it was somewhere at the far end of the Sea of Galilee, somewhere where the feeding of the 5,000 was supposed to have taken place, and all the way up the hill there was nothing but sheep, sheep, sheep.

At the top, above all these sheep, was Christ sitting on a throne. As the picture developed, one of the sheep halfway down started chatting to its neighbour. Christ very graciously came down off his throne, walked all the way down past all the other sheep, came down to this sheep and with great love just took the sheep's face in his hands and very gently turned his face so that he was facing up the mountain again. So that when the picture finished all the sheep in the picture were looking up to Christ.

A Commodious Room

'OUR SOCIETIES', said John Wesley, 'were formed from those who were wandering upon the dark mountains, that belonged to no Christian church; but were awakened by the preaching of the Methodists, who had pursued them through the wilderness of this world to the highways and the hedges, to the markets and the fairs, to the hills and the dales, who set up the standard of the Cross in the streets and the lanes of the cities, in the villages, in the barns and the farmers' kitchens, etc – and all this done in such a way and to such an extent as never to have been done before since the Apostolic age.'

'I love a commodious room,' he added, 'a soft cushion and a handsome pulpit, but field preaching saves souls.'

Let's get back to the adaptability of the Wesleyan era – running Alpha courses in homes, halls, offices, Christian unions, prisons, institutions, mothers and toddlers groups, youth groups and older; in towns, villages, streets and hamlets; any and every sort of group or setting where there are people who don't know Jesus.

An Archbishop's Letter

I CAME ACROSS a letter some years ago that Archbishop William Temple wrote to his son. His son was struggling a little bit at Oxford and experiencing what he called 'philosophical difficulties'. I can't believe that there are many that haven't been through that sort of experience.

The Archbishop wrote back to his son: 'I am obliged to confess (slightly Victorian writing but you will get the drift of what he is saying) that from the years of seventeen to five and twenty I indulged largely in such speculations and philosophical difficulties. But I felt all along like a swimmer who sees no shore before him after long swimming and at last allows himself to be picked up by a ship that seems to be going his way.'

'My passing ship', he wrote, 'was Saint John.'

St John's message is a simple one, but it is the hardest lesson for each of us to learn. It is basically this: that the natural faculties of human beings are insufficient to supply you with what you need.

All through St John's Gospel, you can see all the time (but especially in his early chapters) that he is trying to effect a transition in our minds from the flesh to the Spirit. The things described by John happened as a matter of history of course, but St John's message is: 'Can you see what God is doing through that?'

Put to the Test

IN 1536, HUGH LATIMER, Bishop of Worcester, preached before the Convocation of Canterbury. 'Ye have oft sat in consultation,' he said, 'but what have ye done? Ye have had many things in deliberation, but what one is put forth whereby either Christ is more glorified, or else Christ's people made more holy?'

What would he say today?

How Will They Hear?

SOME YEARS AGO I was on the Board of Visitors at Holloway Prison. I went into a cell one morning. Six young women were in there. On the little green notice-board that one of them had behind her bed was a solitary birthday card pinned open. The message was somewhat stark.

'We wish things could have worked out differently. Much love, Dad.'

The depth of agony and the sense of hopelessness that lay behind that little card can only be imagined.

Many people, despite often having a veneer of so-called independence, are asking real questions; they want real answers. We know that Jesus, and only Jesus, can provide those. But how will they hear?

The Bishop and the Nun

THE FIRST OF OUR CATHOLIC Alpha conferences was opened by Bishop Ambrose Griffiths, who was the Roman Catholic Bishop of Hexham and Newcastle.

When it came to question time, a sweet nun asked one of the first questions.

She said, 'I have listened to all the talks and I have found them quite helpful. But I've not heard a great deal about Mary.'

Bishop Ambrose went to the microphone and said, 'Mary's greatest wish is that we should fall in love with her son Jesus. When we've done that, we'll talk about Mary.'

It was straight from heaven. And he being a bishop and she being a nun, she said simply, 'Oh yes.'

That's what I call a commitment to unity. I want to say we've made so many friends through Alpha with Roman Catholics and others that I wouldn't miss for anything.

Forgiven

AN AMERICAN FRIEND of mine came over here for the first time some years ago. On the Sunday morning she went into an Anglican church for 1662 morning prayer. They said together the General Confession ('to be said of the whole Congregation after the Minister, all kneeling').

'We have erred, and strayed...like lost sheep...followed too much the devices and desires of our own hearts...offended against thy holy laws...there is no health in us...have mercy upon us, miserable offenders...spare...restore...that we may hereafter live a godly, righteous, and sober life...'

She was so impressed. A real spirit of penitence. The minister said the Absolution and she left the church that morning hugely encouraged by the spiritual health of that part of the church she had seen so early in her visit.

That evening she went back for evening prayer. To her astonishment they prayed what seemed like the same prayer all over again! She said to herself: 'What have all these people been doing all afternoon?' Could it be that they didn't know that forgiven means...forgiven?

Alexander Duff

MY ANCESTOR ALEXANDER DUFF was the first missionary to be sent abroad by the Church of Scotland. He went to India and founded a theological college. It is a moving and inspiring story.

Speaking on foreign missions on one of his home leaves here in May 1854, he said this: 'Oh what promises are ours if only we have faith to grasp them! What a promise is that in the great commission – "Go, and do...and lo! I am with you even to the end of the world."

'We go forth amongst the hundreds of millions of the nations, we find gigantic systems of idolatry and superstition consolidated over 3,000 years, heaped up and multiplied for ages upon ages until they tower as high mountains mightier than the Himalayas...but what does faith say? Believe...and it shall be so.'

'And if any church on earth can realise that faith, to that church will the honour belong of evangelising the nations and bringing down the mountains.'

The Man from Turin

AT BISHOP LESSLIE NEWBIGIN'S funeral his son told us that, in his later years, when he couldn't sleep, he took to composing limericks. One of them went like this:

There once was a man from Turin
Who could preach several hours about sin
But as he never left space
To talk about grace,
He never got under my skin.

A Civilised Affair

AS A NEW CURATE in London, I was asked to look after a group of elderly people which met on a regular basis. It was called the Onslow Square Fellowship and it was a very civilised affair. We discussed weighty matters over real coffee out of china cups.

One evening I thought I had given a fascinating talk on the resurrection when one of the ladies said, 'Well, I think he came back as ectoplasm.'

And before I could redirect the discussion to a rather more Biblical line, another dear lady said, 'Oh, how interesting!' and the hare was up and running...

I thought we were lost until, mercifully, the only other gentleman present, who was very deaf, looked up at me and said, *'Do you see much of the Arabs?'* And I decided that was an easier question to answer...

Church home groups have changed a bit since then, I'm thankful to say.

I'll Fight

IN GENERAL BOOTH'S last speech to the Salvation Army, he gave a sort of summary of what drove him on in his lifetime:

> While women weep, as they do now, I'll fight; while little children go hungry, as they do now, I'll fight; while men go to prison, in and out, in and out, as they do now, I'll fight; while there is a drunkard left, while there is a poor lost girl upon the streets, while there remains one dark soul without the light of God, I'll fight – I'll fight to the very end!

And he did. Why shouldn't we?

Missing the Whole Point

HELMUT THIELICKE was a conservative German theologian who preached a lot towards the end of his life at St Michael's Cathedral in Hamburg. He died in 1986.

One of the things that he said was this: 'God will

have to write in red ink beneath the story of many lives, "A remarkable performance. Lively. Interesting. Fascinating. But you missed the whole point." And by that time the story will have ended and cannot be rewritten.'

A Preacher's Advice

I HAVE IN THE BACK of the little looseleaf book I use for preaching, a note that Richard Baxter had in his, and which John Wesley copied into his (the similarity ends there!): 'I preach as never sure to preach again, and as a dying man to dying men.'

Or as Martin Luther once said: 'I live as though Jesus was crucified yesterday, rose this morning and is coming back tomorrow.'

I wonder if we could all say that?

George Whitefield

GEORGE WHITEFIELD USED to make a distinction between preaching to 'churchy' people and preaching to those who knew they were sinners. In prisons he preached endlessly, 'For God so loved the world that he gave his only Son...'

In churchy places he preached deeply and passionately for the fruit of the Spirit, for the marks of salvation, for the signs of having turned, for the desire to make our life useful to other people and to God, turning from our selfishness, to get involved in the kingdom of God, to work in the vineyard.

The Gardener

SOME YEARS AGO, a man, travelling in Sicily, came across a house with a beautifully kept garden. It was in Palermo and was known by the locals as 'the English garden'. Working away in a corner was the gardener. They got talking and the traveller asked him, 'How long have you worked here?'

'Forty years.'

'Is the owner about?'

'He's away but he'll be back.'

'When?'

'I don't know.'

'How long is it since you last saw him?'

'I've never seen him.'

'What an amazing thing! You've worked here for forty years without seeing the owner and you don't know when he's coming back. Why, this place is kept so beautifully. You'd think you were expecting him tomorrow.'

'Today, sir. Today.'[1]

---

[1] I remember telling this story in a talk on Advent Sunday 1976 at Holy Trinity Brompton. Afterwards, one of our older members, Elsa Rogers, came up to me and asked if I had ever been to the garden. I had to confess that I hadn't – I wasn't even sure that it still existed, although I loved the story.

'Oh, certainly!' she said. 'It belonged to the Whittaker family, who made Marsala wine, and was full of the most wonderful flowers that usually only really grow in England, like Cinneraria. A beautiful place.'

Exercising Faith

I AM A GREAT ADMIRER of Oswald Chambers' book, *My Utmost For His Highest*. His strong themes include not just the reflection that God has said, 'Never will I leave you or forsake you' but the faith that responds, 'Therefore I will say, "the Lord is my helper"'. It is one thing to know that God has said, 'Never will I leave you or forsake you,' it is another to respond and exercise faith in that response.

Oswald Chambers points out that faith rides high when we're on an exciting new venture for God, but it's not so easy when you're just living from day to day. But it's in the ordinary things of life, as Oswald says strongly, that God actually reveals himself.

Overcrowding in the Nineteenth Century

LORD SHAFTESBURY told of a visit he made to a slum in North London. Having been informed that five families lived together in one room, a family in each corner and one in the middle, he asked how they managed it. 'Oh,' came the reply, 'we did very well until the family in the middle took in a lodger.'

An Army is Born

THERE IS A LOVELY account of William Booth staying with his friends, the Palmers, in Walsall in 1863. His converts had already started the 'Hallelujah Band' and it was through their ministry that Booth adopted a lasting principle that the masses would be reached most effectively by their 'own kind'. Booth spent all day walking up and down in the Palmers' garden, with his head on his chest, clearly deep in thought.

At the end of the afternoon Palmer asked him what had been going on. Booth, apparently with his face shining, replied, 'My friend, I am thinking out a plan, which, when it is implemented, will mean blessing to the whole wide world.'

And so the Salvation Army was born.

We're Christians

I WAS READING an article by the evangelist Tony Campolo in *Christianity and Renewal* magazine. He said he was sitting in a café recently and somebody started to speak to him. They asked him what he was and he said with some degree of pride, 'I am an evangelical Christian.'

And he saw a look on the face of the person listening to him. I think I can imagine it. Well, you can too – a sort of hunted look. It had such an effect on Tony that he vowed never to call himself an evangelical again.

I come from an evangelical tradition but I don't like the words 'evangelical' or 'charismatic'. I don't like any sort of word now that adds to 'Christian' because the Spirit of God is uniting us all in a way that I don't think was happening ten years ago.

There are Christians in every sort of denomination and tradition now and there is only one word for what they are: *Christians*.

Do it Again, Lord

THERE IS AN ACCOUNT of William Booth's funeral which tells of a scene when the coffin had been taken out and the church was very nearly empty.

Just one lonely figure was kneeling at the front rail and as the verger hovered, waiting to lock up, he heard the kneeling man tapping the rail with clenched fists and praying with passion, 'Lord, do it again...do it again.'

The Best Way to Belief

THERE ARE REALLY only two ways of approaching belief. We can wait until we understand in order to believe or we can decide to believe in order that we can begin to understand. These two are not necessarily irreconcilable, but they are not easy to do together.

Much of modern study today assumes that we must first understand if we are going to be able to believe. But that assumption carries with it great risk. The risk is that if we are to find God we have to take a step of faith, a step which may never be taken if we insist on waiting until we can properly understand. 'Faith', said Kierkegaard, 'wants to state the absolute, whereas reason wants to continue to reflect.'

But the resurrection is beyond human understanding. It is the mysterious work of God – divine omnipotence. We humans can't do resurrection – that is the point. Only God can. So if we continually postpone belief until we 'understand' we shall never believe. The problem is compounded because we tend to want to be in charge of the whole process.

While we are seeking truth *we* are in charge. When the truth is acknowledged – *he* is in charge! As Bono put it in his song, 'Walk on, Walk on': 'You're packing a suitcase for a place none of us has been; a place that has to be believed to be seen.'

So the best way to faith is to take a deep breath and dare to believe.

The Issue is Salvation

HOW CAN WE – how can you and I – get right with God? The varying degrees of evil in the world leave us totally unqualified for heaven. Without some sort of divine intervention we are destined to live our lives here separated from God, and permanently so in the hereafter.

How awful to be permanently separated from God and from everything that is precious and pure, beautiful, kind; from friendship and relationship; from music and art; from joy and peace.

Some years ago I found myself at Gatwick trying, along with several hundred others, to fly off on holiday with my family. Planes were being cancelled, desks closed, queues of people changing from one line to another, trying to get information.

An old friend whom I hadn't seen since I got ordained suddenly appeared beside me. Casting his eyes to the ceiling, he said, 'Please assure me that hell will not be as bad as this.'

I said, 'I'm so sorry – it will be worse, and permanent.'

Jesus teaches, 'God so loved the world that he gave his one and only Son, that whoever believes in him shall not perish but have eternal life. For God did not send his Son into the world to condemn the world, but to save the world through him.' (John 3:16-17)

So the issue is...salvation. Paul expressly teaches that salvation depends on faith in the resurrection of Jesus.[1] And he also makes clear that belief in the bodily resurrection of Jesus is not an appendage to the Christian faith – it is the Christian faith.[2]

This is why it is always so inspiring to read the enthusiasm with which the news of the resurrection was imparted on that first Sunday morning.

'Don't be alarmed; you are looking for Jesus the Nazarene, who was crucified. He has risen! He is not here.' (Mark 16:6)

'Why do you look for the living among the dead? He is not here; he has risen!' (Luke 24:5-6)

It is such a powerful message.

And so the Word went out on its long journey through history, spreading the good news throughout all the earth, unstoppable until the end of time, when Jesus will appear again in power and glory to judge the world.

[1] In his letter to the Romans
[2] In 1 Corinthians 15

Preaching with Faith

THERE WAS a young man who once said to the nineteenth century Baptist minister, Charles Spurgeon, 'Why is it that whenever I preach, nobody's converted?'

Spurgeon replied, 'Surely you don't expect someone to be converted each time you preach?'

'No, I don't...'

'Well,' he said, 'that's why.'

The End of the Road

But one thing I do. Forgetting what is behind and straining towards what is ahead I press on towards the goal to win the prize for which God has called me heavenwards in Christ Jesus.

Philippians 3:13

ST PAUL SAW MORE clearly than many of us that Jesus had taken hold of him for a purpose. The emphasis is not that we have given our lives to Jesus – it is that he has a plan for them.

I was brought up to love the songs of Harry Lauder, the first knight of the old music hall, who died in 1950.

He came from a very poor but God-fearing family. His father died when he was eleven, at which moment he became the breadwinner for his widowed mother and her six younger children.

Perhaps his best known song now is, 'Keep right on to the end of the road'. He composed it after hearing that his only son John, whom he adored, had been killed in France on New Year's Day 1917. John's last words were said to have been, 'Carry on.' That same evening Harry was on the stage singing that song he had composed.

The audience was only told at the end of the performance – my grandmother was amongst them – and it made an unforgettable impression of courage and determination.

Keep right on to the end of the road,
Keep right on to the end,
Tho' the way be long, let your heart be strong,
Keep right on round the bend.
Tho' you're tired and weary still journey on,
Till you come to your happy abode,
Where all the love you've been dreaming of
Will be there at the end of the road.

It could have been written by St Paul.

Building a Kingdom

WHEN SIR CHRISTOPHER WREN was visiting St Paul's Cathedral in the seventeenth century, he found three men doing exactly the same job – shaping a bit of stone. He went up to each of them unannounced. He said to the first one, 'Do tell me, what are you doing?'

The man replied, 'Well, I am shaping this stone. I want to make it into an arch.'

He said to the second man who was at the next door place, 'What are you doing?'

He replied, 'I'm building the East window.'

So he went to the third one who was doing the same thing. 'What are you doing?' he said.

'I'm building a cathedral.'

We are all involved together in building the kingdom of God, but we may have different visions of the part we play.

The Church of Today

SOME TIME, in some place, there has to be a body of people who are committed to living out the life of Christ in sincere and pure devotion to him, reaching out to the people of the world in his name to offer them not criticism, but a better way of life and an unconditional love through an incomparable Saviour. They have traditionally been called the Church. In this generation why shouldn't they be us?

A Prayer

I very much hope that some reading this book will want to explore further some aspects of the Christian faith and I'd love to encourage you to do an Alpha course as a start. But there may be some of you who would like to pray to invite the Spirit of God into your heart now. At that moment we become a new creature at the start of its journey. I often say that we don't put babies out in the garden to see if they will grow...

We feed them and encourage them – through reading the Bible, through prayer and Christian fellowship. But it starts at that moment when you ask the Spirit of God into your spirit. If you would like to do this, why don't you pray this prayer, now:

Lord Jesus Christ, thank you for dying for me. Thank you for your promise that whoever comes to you, you will never turn away. I ask you to forgive me for the past, to fill me with your Holy Spirit and to enable me to know in my deepest being that I am born from above, because you have come to live in me. Thank you Lord. Amen.

If you have prayed that prayer, however falteringly, I'd love to encourage you to join an Alpha course which will help you to grow. There's bound to be one near you and God is using Alpha now all over the world to help thousands to know him and grow in his love.